WEEPING
and
GNASHING

Eternal Points of Regret

DAG HEWARD-MILLS

Parchment House

Unless otherwise stated, all Scripture quotations are taken from the King James Version of the Bible.

WEEPING AND GNASHING

Copyright © 2022 Dag Heward-Mills

First published 2022 by Parchment House

[77]Find out more about Dag Heward-Mills at:

Healing Jesus Campaign
Email: evangelist@daghewardmills.org
Website: www.daghewardmills.org
Facebook: Dag Heward-Mills
Twitter: @EvangelistDag

ISBN : 978-1-64330-277-5

Contents

CHAPTER 1

What is Weeping and Gnashing?

And they shall make themselves utterly bald for thee, and gird them with sackcloth, and THEY SHALL WEEP FOR THEE with bitterness of heart and bitter wailing.

Ezekiel 27:31

Weeping and gnashing of teeth is to grind teeth together in rage, pain, frustration and disappointment. Many people will be disappointed in eternity, having wasted the opportunities that came to them on earth.

The phrase "weeping and gnashing" appears five times in the Bible. Jesus used this phrase on five different occasions. He was trying to give us a glimpse of the deep sense of loss and regret some people will feel when they get to heaven.

When they heard these things, they were cut to the heart, and THEY GNASHED on him with their teeth.

Acts 7:54

The term "weeping and gnashing" is a prophetic warning about eternal points of regret. The prophecies of this terrible event are a prophetic warning about the pain, the anger, the sorrow, the regret, the remorse and the sense of loss that will be felt on getting into heaven without being ready for it.

All those who end up weeping and gnashing their teeth will miss out on something important. They will miss eternal rewards they could have had! They will miss the joy they would have had and they will miss the crowns of glory.

You must do whatever you can to avoid becoming one of the people who will be weeping and gnashing their teeth in regret.

Weeping and Gnashing in School

When I speak about regret, I always remember the story of one of my pastors who took an exam when he was in secondary school. This was a final exam and a very important one at that. The instructions for the exam were clear: "*Answer Question One and Four Other Questions.*" However, my friend thought that the instructions were "Answer Question One and Three Other questions" making a total of four. Somehow, the words "Question One" and the total number of "4" were stuck in his head.

After the exam, the young man was discussing with his friends and found out that it was actually Question One and Four Other questions. He was alarmed and feared greatly that he would fail the exam because he had left out a whole question. He could not believe that he had made such a foolish mistake because the question that he had left out would actually have been very easy for him to do. He would have had full marks if he had answered that other question. The young man was left weeping and gnashing his teeth in regret for not reading the instructions properly.

Indeed, these moments of regret, where you cannot go back and do what you could have done are terrible moments of weeping and gnashing.

You must never need to say, "I want to go back to earth to do what I didn't do."

[1]You see, life is so short! It passes so quickly and soon it is gone. You just have one life to live on earth, so remember your Creator while you have breath! You only have one life to live on earth.[1] Before you know it, it's come and gone. So make the most of it while you can! And remember your Creator whilst you have breath!

The Vision

I remember a vision I had. In this vision, two men came to visit me in my house. The men, who were brothers, had died years ago and had been brought back to life and given a chance to revisit the earth.

In the vision, I found myself sitting at a dining table with the two dead pastors who had come back to life for a short period. During this short visit, they went round some churches they had established in their lifetime and tried to minister in them.

[1-1] Lyrics, *Life is Short* by Bernice Offei: *"LIFE"* 2018

As we ate and shared fellowship, I asked them how they had found the churches they had visited. They said they were unhappy because their messages were not received in the churches anymore. When they had been on earth they had also composed many songs. They realized on this visit that no one wanted to sing their songs anymore.

These two dead brothers were disappointed that their visit had virtually no impact on the people they had ministered to in their lifetime. The brothers told me three important things that I never forgot.

1. They told me that they were very surprised when they died. They did not expect to die when they did because they were very fruitful in ministry and presumed that was a good reason for them to live much longer.

2. Yet another thing that surprised them was the fact that they had no impact at all on the people during their visit to earth. The people did not even notice them.

3. They also told me, "You have the best chance now. This is your time to be fruitful. Our time is past. Our chance is gone. This is your best chance; now!"

The vision ended and I realized that God had spoken to me. It was clear that I could depart from this earth at any time in spite of the good works I was doing.

God had told me that this was my chance to do His will and to finish His work. You can best impact your generation whilst you are alive. Dead people are quickly forgotten. These men wanted to come back to the earth but could not. We will not be able to come to the earth. We will regret deeply not doing anything that we should have done for the Lord whilst we were on earth.

This book about weeping and gnashing is an effort to keep us from regretting our time on earth. There is so much trouble on this earth. We really need to enjoy heaven. If you start your life in heaven with weeping and gnashing, heaven may not be as joyful as you anticipate.

The Speed Cameras

One day, I visited a country which had many cameras on the streets to take photographs of over-speeding cars. The cameras were simply everywhere and it was very easy to be photographed and receive a ticket for speeding. The friend who was driving me around told me that he had a map of the city that showed where every camera was located. "How clever he was," I thought.

Then he told me, "This map which shows the location of all the cameras is something that is available to the public."

The police were actually trying to help people to avoid being fined. They were giving out these maps to help people to avoid being photographed and caught in a trap. I thought to myself, "How kind these policemen are."

This is exactly what Jesus has done for us. He has given us a map showing us exactly what will get us into trouble on the Judgment Day. He has shown us the things that will make us end our race with weeping and gnashing of teeth. We have ourselves to blame if we ignore these clear warnings about what will give us grief on Judgment Day.

CHAPTER 2

The First Prophecy of Weeping and Gnashing

And when Jesus was entered into Capernaum, there came unto him a centurion, beseeching him, And saying, Lord, my servant lieth at home sick of the palsy, grievously tormented.

And Jesus saith unto him, I will come and heal him.

The centurion answered and said, Lord, I am not worthy that thou shouldest come under my roof: but speak the word only, and my servant shall be healed.

For I am a man under authority, having soldiers under me: and I say to this man, Go, and he goeth; and to another, Come, and he cometh; and to my servant, Do this, and he doeth it.

When Jesus heard it, he marvelled, and said to them that followed, Verily I say unto you, I have not found so great faith, no, not in Israel.

And I say unto you, that many shall come from the east and west, and shall sit down with Abraham, and Isaac, and Jacob, in the kingdom of heaven.

But the children of the kingdom shall be cast out into outer darkness: THERE SHALL BE WEEPING AND GNASHING OF TEETH.

And Jesus said unto the centurion, Go thy way; and as thou hast believed, so be it done unto thee. And his servant was healed in the selfsame hour.

Matthew 8:5-13

1. **You will eternally regret that you were too familiar with the great men who were given to you on earth, to appreciate them.**

You will regret not recognizing God's servants! In the story above, Jesus gives us some points of regret that will meet everyone who enters eternity. Jesus' encounter with the centurion made Him prophesy that there would be weeping and gnashing of teeth. The prophecy of weeping and gnashing is a prediction that there would be something that would cause great regret.

Jesus was sent into this world. He came to the Jews but they did not appreciate Him. It was a centurion from the Roman Empire who recognized how great Jesus was and the kind of authority He was carrying. Jesus prophesied that people would regret not recognizing Him. They would regret not recognizing the kind of person that walked in their midst.

You will also eternally regret that you were close but could not recognize and acknowledge men of God sent into your life. Everyone has the experience of someone being sent to him. Most of the time, people do not appreciate great men who are sent to them. There is so much you can benefit from God's servants. There is so much power available. There is so much revelation available. There is so much God wants to do for you through His servants. Will God's men pass through your life without you recognizing who they are? Will you insult, blaspheme, criticize and accuse them? Will you honour them and believe in them when they are practically present with you?

> **And I say unto you, that many shall come from the east and west, and shall sit down with Abraham, and Isaac, and Jacob, in the kingdom of heaven. But the children of the kingdom shall be cast out into outer darkness: there shall be weeping and gnashing of teeth.**
>
> **Matthew 8:11-12**

2. You will eternally regret that you did not have great faith, great beliefs and great obedience like the centurion did.

When Jesus heard it, he marvelled, and said to them that followed, Verily I say unto you, I HAVE NOT FOUND SO GREAT FAITH, no, not in Israel. And I say unto you, that many shall come from the east and west, and shall sit down with Abraham, and Isaac, and Jacob, in the kingdom of heaven. But the children of the kingdom shall be cast out into outer darkness: THERE SHALL BE WEEPING AND GNASHING OF TEETH.

Matthew 8:10-12

You will regret not having great faith! Jesus was sent into this world. He did many signs and wonders and He preached amazing messages to the world. He raised the dead! He healed the sick and He opened the eyes of the blind. Yet, many people did not really believe in Him. Many people did not have great faith in Him. Then came a centurion from the Roman Empire who had great faith in Jesus Christ. Jesus was shocked at the man's faith.

Jesus was amazed that someone who was not a Jew had such great beliefs. Jesus taught us that in eternity many would regret not believing in the word of God, as they should have. Many believers agree with the word of God. They give mental assent to the things that God says.

But it is important to have great faith and great beliefs. To have great faith is to greatly believe in certain things. I think there are many pastors that do not really believe in heaven. If they did, they would live differently and serve God more fervently. Many pastors do not have great beliefs about hell. If they did, they would preach the gospel that Jesus preached and warn people about hell.

Jesus predicted that in heaven there would be regret of the fact that we did not greatly believe in His words and His warnings.

3. You will eternally regret that you did not recognize great spiritual authority like this centurion did.

FOR I AM A MAN UNDER AUTHORITY, having soldiers under me: and I say to this man, Go, and he goeth; and to another, Come, and he cometh; and to my servant, Do this, and he doeth it.

When Jesus heard it, he marvelled, and said to them that followed, Verily I say unto you, I have not found so great faith, no, not in Israel.

And I say unto you, that many shall come from the east and west, and shall sit down with Abraham, and Isaac, and Jacob, in the kingdom of heaven.

But the children of the kingdom shall be cast out into outer darkness: THERE SHALL BE WEEPING AND GNASHING OF TEETH.

And Jesus said unto the centurion, Go thy way; and as thou hast believed, so be it done unto thee. And his servant was healed in the selfsame hour.

Matthew 8:9-13

There are different levels of authority in the kingdom. Some pastors have greater authority than others. It is important to recognize authority in the kingdom. When I became a doctor, I took an oath that said, "I will respect my teachers." There are many people who are medical doctors. However, there are some medical doctors who are great men of authority in their special fields.

A novice doctor must be able to recognize senior and experienced authorities in the different medical fields. In the same way, it is important for pastors to recognize different authorities in different fields.

The centurion recognized Jesus' authority. He realized that Jesus was somebody who could give commands and many people would obey. Just a Word from Jesus would cause many things to be set in motion. That is great authority! You must distinguish between men of great authority and novices. You must distinguish between pastors who are just sharing nice ideas from the pulpit and men who wield great authority.

Jesus taught that there would be eternal regret for not recognizing men of great authority. All through my life, God has led me to men of great spiritual authority. Most of my mentors have been men of great spiritual authority.

I am hardly attracted to perfect gentlemen in the ministry. Many of these neat, perfect-looking gentlemen are not men of authority. They may have logical points and ideas to share; but that is not what we need! A man of authority is a man who has been through a war. He has wounds! He has scars! He has stories! He has testimonies! He has near escapes! He has life and death stories! He has lots of enemies! He has many who love him and many who hate him.

All these make up a man of authority. You cannot have authority unless you have been through the pain, the fire, the tribulations and the temptations. You must pay attention to such people when they preach and teach. You will receive a whole wealth of knowledge that you will not get when you listen to novices speaking. Do not miss the great opportunities with a man of authority!

4. **You will eternally regret that you did not recognize the church as a militarized organization like this centurion did.**

The centurion recognized Jesus' military role and rank. The Jews to whom Jesus had been sent, did not recognize Jesus' rank. They did not even recognize that the kingdom of God operated with many military concepts such as the importance of rank.

The centurion also recognized that even though Jesus was a spiritual person, the concept of rank, taking orders and military discipline, were very much a part of spiritual authority. Today, many Christians do not recognize the importance of taking orders, respecting spiritual rank and the need for discipline.

Without these concepts working in the church, it becomes ineffective. Today, the church is more like a large Sunday school with many toddlers and crying babies. Everybody wants a toy and everybody wants to play games. But no one wants to get to the serious job of fighting the enemy, overpowering evil, overcoming darkness and building the church.

You will eternally regret that you did not see the church as a military organization, which is what it is. You will eternally regret that you did not build your church as a military organization.

You will eternally regret not dealing with the enemy in a militarized and merciless fashion. Satan has organized demon forces into hordes and groups with commanders and princes over them. What chance do we have when we come against satan's organized army? What chance would we have if we came against the enemy as a large group of cry babies and spoilt children?

Military means rank. Military means take orders and follow them till new orders come. Jesus gave us marching orders to go into the world and preach the gospel. We have refused to act like a disciplined army. We have refused to carry out our orders even though no new order has come forth.

We have shied away from the real battle. We have shied away from real missions. We have bowed out of true ministry and gone into games. All pastors want toys like cars, houses, silver and gold. Pastors want to have get-togethers, weddings, funerals and a thousand celebrations that contribute nothing to the military instructions that we have received from our military commander. Jesus is our military commander. It was the centurion who recognized this reality. Let us build militarized churches so that we will not regret it on Judgment Day!

For I am a man under authority, HAVING SOLDIERS UNDER ME: and I say to this man, Go, and he goeth; and to another, Come, and he cometh; and to my servant, Do this, and he doeth it.

When Jesus heard it, he marvelled, and said to them that followed, Verily I say unto you, I have not found so great faith, no, not in Israel.

And I say unto you, that many shall come from the east and west, and shall sit down with Abraham, and Isaac, and Jacob, in the kingdom of heaven.

But the children of the kingdom shall be cast out into outer darkness: there shall be weeping and gnashing of teeth.

And Jesus said unto the centurion, Go thy way; and as thou hast believed, so be it done unto thee. And his servant was healed in the selfsame hour.

Matthew 8:9-13

CHAPTER 3

The Second Prophecy of Weeping and Gnashing

The kingdom of heaven is like unto a certain king, which made a marriage for his son, And sent forth his servants to call them that were bidden to the wedding: and they would not come. Again, he sent forth other servants, saying, Tell them which are bidden, Behold, I have prepared my dinner: my oxen and my fatlings are killed, and all things are ready: come unto the marriage. But they made light of it, and went their ways, one to his farm, another to his merchandise: And the remnant took his servants, and entreated them spitefully, and slew them.

But when the king heard thereof, he was wroth: and he sent forth his armies, and destroyed those murderers, and burned up their city. Then saith he to his servants, the wedding is ready, but they which were bidden were not worthy. Go ye therefore into the highways, and as many as ye shall find, bid to the marriage.

So those servants went out into the highways, and gathered together all as many as they found, both bad and good: and the wedding was furnished with guests. And when the king came in to see the guests, he saw there a man which had not on a wedding garment: And he saith unto him, Friend, how camest thou in hither not having a wedding garment?

And he was speechless. Then said the king to the servants, Bind him hand and foot, and take him away, and cast him into outer darkness; THERE SHALL BE WEEPING AND GNASHING OF TEETH. For many are called, but few are chosen.

Matthew 22:2-14

1. **You will eternally regret that you were among the many who were called but not among the few who were chosen.**

The kingdom of heaven is like unto a certain king, which made a marriage for his son, and sent forth his servants to call them that were bidden to the wedding: and they would not come.

Again, he sent forth other servants, saying, Tell them which are bidden, Behold, I have prepared my dinner: my oxen and my fatlings are killed, and all things are ready: come unto the marriage.

But they made light of it, and went their ways, one to his farm, another to his merchandise:

Matthew 22:2-5

In this story, we see how many people were invited to a party. Instead of many people attending the party, just a few showed up. Many took the invitation lightly! Many went their own ways; some to the farm and others to their merchandise. In the same way, many people have been invited to God's kingdom. Many people have been called to the ministry. Many people have been specially selected to serve God in various capacities.

Unfortunately, few people respond properly to this great invitation. Jesus prophesied that there will be weeping and gnashing of teeth over this point. Jesus predicted that people would regret not taking the call of God seriously. Jesus predicted that people would regret not being among the few who were chosen.

You will regret for the whole of eternity that you did not take the call of God with the seriousness that it deserved. You set God aside and told Him that He was disposable and expendable. God does not like to be disposable. Nor does He like to be expendable. God is the first! He will always want the first position. You must pay attention to God because He wants it and deserves it.

2. You will eternally regret that you did not adjust to the call by putting on the clothes of righteousness.

And he saith unto him, Friend, how camest thou in hither not having a wedding garment? And he was speechless. Then said the king to the servants, Bind him hand and foot, and take him away, and cast him into outer darkness; THERE SHALL BE WEEPING AND GNASHING OF TEETH. For many are called, but few are chosen.

Matthew 22:12-14

Many people who are called by God do not adjust their lives to the call of God. It is great to have a call of God. You will have to adjust yourself to God's conditions. God will not accept us anyhow.

In this story, Jesus showed us how a guest was thrown out because he was not properly dressed.   Jesus prophesied that people would be thrown out of the kingdom because they were not properly dressed.

When you go to many golf courses you will find rules and regulations on how to dress on the golf course. Golf courses do not accept people coming around and dressing just anyhow. There are many hotels that also do not allow people to dress anyhow in their lobbies and restaurants. Your poor dressing will degrade and demean the image of the hotel or the golf course.

Similarly, your poor dressing will demean and degrade the kingdom of God. Your dressing speaks of your righteousness in God.

I will greatly rejoice in the Lord, my soul shall be joyful in my God; for he hath clothed me with the garments of salvation, he hath COVERED ME WITH THE ROBE OF RIGHTEOUSNESS, as a bridegroom decketh himself with ornaments, and as a bride adorneth herself with her jewels.

Isaiah 61:10

Your dressing also speaks of humility. As a servant of God, you are expected to be clothed with humility.

Likewise, ye younger, submit yourselves unto the elder. Yea, all of you be subject one to another, and BE CLOTHED WITH HUMILITY: for God resisteth the proud, and giveth grace to the humble.

1 Peter 5:5

Jesus was therefore prophesying about righteousness and humility. Jesus was predicting that there would be regret in heaven because we did not walk in righteousness and humility.

Righteousness will involve serious adjustments and adaptations to your life. You will have to dissociate from wicked practices and evil things. You may have to cut off an arm or a leg so that you can be free to serve in the kingdom. If you are not prepared to do this, you will not qualify for the kingdom. Unfortunately, Jesus predicted that many would not be prepared to pay the price for the clothes of righteousness.

To have the cloak of humility, you have to lower yourself and walk in meekness. Walking in forgiveness means you have put on the cloak of humility. Walking without arrogance and overconfidence is a sign that you have put on the cloak of humility. Living without contention and quarrels with other people is a sign that you have put on the cloak of humility. This is because the Bible says, "Only by pride cometh contention..." (Proverbs 13:10).

It is time to put on the cloak of humility and walk in meekness and lowliness of mind, not esteeming yourself better than any other (Philippians 2:3).

When you have the cloak of humility, you will do great things for God and become accepted by the Father. All traces of pride are traces of satan.

All traces of pride are traces of demonic infestation. Satan is filled with pride, arrogance and rebellion.

Thousands of years have gone by since his rebellion but he is still filled with pride, arrogance and anger. Any cloak that has threads and patterns of pride, arrogance or rebellion will not be compatible with God's kingdom.

CHAPTER 4

The Third Prophecy of Weeping and Gnashing

But know this, that if the goodman of the house had known in what watch the thief would come, he would have watched, and would not have suffered his house to be broken up.

Therefore be ye also ready: for in such an hour as ye think not the Son of man cometh. WHO THEN IS A FAITHFUL AND WISE SERVANT, whom his lord hath made ruler over his household, to give them meat in due season? Blessed is that servant, whom his lord when he cometh shall find so doing.

Verily I say unto you, That he shall make him ruler over all his goods. But and if that evil servant shall say in his heart, My lord delayeth his coming; And shall begin to smite his fellowservants, and to eat and drink with the drunken; The lord of that servant shall come in a day when he looketh not for him , and in an hour that he is not aware of, And shall cut him asunder, and appoint him his portion with the hypocrites: THERE SHALL BE WEEPING AND GNASHING OF TEETH.

Matthew 24:43-51

J esus was specific about why there would be weeping and gnashing of teeth. Weeping and gnashing of teeth is not just a phrase found in the Bible. It is the pointing out of serious and eternal regret for those who do not take their calling seriously. In this chapter, we see how Jesus predicted that there would be weeping and gnashing for those servants who mishandled the call of God. Let us look at why some people will be weeping and gnashing their teeth.

1. You will eternally regret not being wise with your assignment.

WHO THEN IS A FAITHFUL AND WISE SERVANT, whom his lord hath made ruler over his household, to give them meat in due season? Blessed is that servant, whom his lord when he cometh shall find so doing.

Matthew 24:45-46

Jesus predicted that there would be weeping and gnashing for those who were not wise about the call of God. You must apply wisdom to the call of God. When you apply wisdom to the call of God, you bear more fruit. When you apply wisdom to the call of God your fruits will abide.

God expects you to use wisdom in serving Him. When we started having crusades, we would travel to a distant town and spend three days there, preaching the word of God.

Then we would come all the way back and go again for another three days of preaching. One day, I felt the need to apply the wisdom of God to the ministry.

Through the use of new technology, we were able to spend several weeks conducting a series of campaigns without journeying back home. Today, we cannot imagine travelling all the way to these distant locations just to have a three-day campaign. We bore much more fruit in a short while and won more souls with less effort. Applying wisdom makes you bear more fruit. You will regret that you did not apply wisdom to the call that God gave you!

The Wisdom of Paul

Apostle Paul often applied wisdom to what God called him to do. Ministry without wisdom will always result in failure! He knew that he was called to be a supernatural apostle but he still used the wisdom of God.

1. There were times Paul would escape from cities at night. It was wise to run away at night so that's what he did.

   And the brethren immediately sent away Paul and Silas by night unto Berea: who coming thither went into the synagogue of the Jews.

   Acts 17:10

2. There were other times where he would leave his team behind and disappear so that they would catch up with him later.

   And then immediately the brethren sent away Paul to go as it were to the sea: but Silas and Timotheus abode there still.

   Acts 17:14

3. There were times he applied his Roman citizenship to his advantage. All these were acts of wisdom to help him fulfil his ministry.

   But Paul said unto them, they have beaten us openly uncondemned, being Romans, and have cast us into prison; and now do they thrust us out privily? Nay verily; but let them come themselves and fetch us out.

   Acts 16:37

4. On another occasion, Paul personally circumcised his disciple to prevent a crisis from arising if he was seen in the bathroom.

Remember that it is this same Paul who had resisted Peter's attempt to have Titus circumcised because it was against their faith. It seems that Paul personally circumcised Timothy. Imagine that Paul became a surgeon just as an act of wisdom.

Then came he to Derbe and Lystra: and, behold, a certain disciple was there, named Timotheus, the son of a certain woman, which was a Jewess, and believed; but his father was a Greek: Which was well reported of by the brethren that were at Lystra and Iconium. Him would Paul have to go forth with him; and took and circumcised him because of the Jews which were in those quarters: for they knew all that his father was a Greek.

Acts 16:1-3

2. **You will eternally regret not continuing with your assignment faithfully, constantly, unchangingly and not veering off into other things.**

Who then is a faithful and wise servant, whom his lord hath made ruler over his household, to give them meat in due season? Blessed is that servant, whom his lord when he cometh shall find so doing.

Matthew 24:45-46

Jesus predicted that there would be a lot of regret concerning our faithfulness to our calling as servants of God. Faithfulness has to do with being constant, being repetitive and doing monotonous hard work. Many people are not faithful or persistent. Without being faithful you will not achieve the will of God.

Are you faithful? Are you constant? Are you loyal? If you are not faithful, you will regret it.

You must serve God with faithfulness. Remember the words, "Well done, good and FAITHFUL servant."

3. **You will eternally regret thinking "the Lord delayeth His coming".**

    Verily I say unto you, that he shall make him ruler over all his goods. But and if that evil servant shall say in his heart, My lord delayeth his coming; And shall begin to smite his fellowservants, and to eat and drink with the drunken;

    Matthew 24:47-49

    Jesus predicted that there would be weeping and gnashing of teeth because people would think that His return was not imminent. You will regret thinking that the Lord has delayed His return! You will regret feeling that the return of the Lord is not real!

    The coming of the Lord is real. Jesus will return to the earth and set up His kingdom. The kingdoms of this world will become the kingdoms of our Lord.

    Do not set aside the reality of the return of Jesus Christ.

4. **You will eternally regret not giving the right word and meat to your congregations and also regret not giving it in time.**

    Who then is a faithful and wise servant, whom his lord hath made ruler over his household, to give them meat in due season? Blessed is that servant, whom his lord when he cometh shall find so doing.

    Matthew 24:45-46

    It is important to give the right word of God to the congregation. The word of God must be given in season, which means in the right time. God expects you to preach certain messages by a certain time. You cannot just do what you want.

    You cannot do things when you want to do them. I have noticed that certain books and materials must be produced by a certain time. When they come later, they are almost useless.

There are certain things I would not write in the same way today. I am therefore glad I wrote them when I did.

It is important to release the teachings in due season. The Lord expects us to release His Word in due season. What is the point of waiting for a meal from ten o'clock in the morning till seven o'clock in the evening? Nine hours of waiting for breakfast will definitely leave you angry and frustrated.

5. You will eternally regret attacking other Christians, churches and attempts at church work.

But and if that evil servant shall say in his heart, My lord delayeth his coming; And shall begin to SMITE HIS FELLOWSERVANTS, and to eat and drink with the drunken; The lord of that servant shall come in a day when he looketh not for him, and in an hour that he is not aware of, And shall cut him asunder, and appoint him his portion with the hypocrites: THERE SHALL BE WEEPING AND GNASHING OF TEETH.

Matthew 24:48-51

Many Christians attack their fellow Christians. Pastors quarrel with other pastors over various things. Pastors try to pull each other down. It is as though the destruction of a fellow pastor will lead to your success. But that is not the case! Be careful what you say about any other church!

The Catholic Church is a fellow servant and also the parent of all other churches. Be careful that you do not criticise your parents. All other churches are fellow servants. Be careful that you do not smite them. Jesus predicted that there would be great regret for having smitten your fellow servants.

6. You will eternally regret being a hypocrite. You will eternally regret being a pretender.

And shall begin to smite his fellowservants, and to eat and drink with the drunken; The lord of that servant shall come in a day when he looketh not for him, and in an hour that he is not aware of, And shall cut him asunder, AND APPOINT HIM HIS PORTION WITH THE HYPOCRITES: THERE SHALL BE WEEPING AND GNASHING OF TEETH.

Matthew 24:49-51

Hypocrisy will be rewarded with a terrible punishment in heaven. Jesus sees right through your pretences. Unfortunately, man cannot see beyond what you show him. We are all subject to judging from outward appearances. Because of this, many people take advantage and become two-faced and double-sided. Many Christians have two lives. Many Christians are impressive on the outside but are like dead men's tombs on the inside.

Jesus is warning that a terrible punishment awaits those who fool their neighbour with pretence and hypocrisy. Judas was the quintessential hypocrite. He was a friend of Jesus and also a friend of the Pharisees.

He was seemingly a lover of God but also a lover of money. This kind of hypocrisy is what leads to explosive revelations and judgment of the hypocrites in our midst.

Beware of double-sidedness, double-facedness, duality and doubleness. Jesus said hypocrites would weep and gnash their teeth!

7. **You will eternally regret not being alert and on guard always, just as you would regret not being alert to avoid being robbed.**

WATCH THEREFORE: for ye know not what hour your Lord doth come. But know this, that if the goodman of the house had known in what watch the thief would come, he would have watched, and would not have suffered his house to be broken up. Therefore be ye also ready: for in such an hour as ye think not the Son of man cometh.

Matthew 24:42-44

Christians have a tendency to relax and to forget that there is a need to be vigilant. Many Christians are only vigilant during their beginning of year, twenty-one day fast. Jesus warned us to be alert, to be sober and to be vigilant. Jesus prophesied that a lack of alertness and a lack of vigilance would be a reason for eternal regret.

CHAPTER 5

The Fourth Prophecy of Weeping and Gnashing

For the kingdom of heaven is as a man travelling into a far country, who called his own servants, and delivered unto them his goods.

And unto one he gave five talents, to another two, and to another one; to every man according to his several ability; and straightway took his journey.

Then he that had received the five talents went and traded with the same, and made them other five talents.

And likewise he that had received two, he also gained other two.

But he that had received one went and digged in the earth, and hid his lord's money.

After a long time the lord of those servants cometh, and reckoneth with them.

And so he that had received five talents came and brought other five talents, saying, Lord, thou deliveredst unto me five talents: behold, I have gained beside them five talents more.

His lord said unto him, Well done, thou good and faithful servant: thou hast been faithful over a few things, I will make thee ruler over many things: enter thou into the joy of thy lord.

He also that had received two talents came and said, Lord, thou deliveredst unto me two talents: behold, I have gained two other talents beside them.

His lord said unto him, Well done, good and faithful servant; thou hast been faithful over a few things, I will make thee ruler over many things: enter thou into the joy of thy lord.

Then he which had received the one talent came and said, Lord, I knew thee that thou art an hard man, reaping where thou hast not sown, and gathering where thou hast not strawed: And I was afraid, and went and hid thy talent in the earth: lo, there thou hast that is thine.

His lord answered and said unto him, Thou wicked and slothful servant, thou knewest that I reap where I sowed not, and gather where I have not strawed:

Thou oughtest therefore to have put my money to the exchangers, and then at my coming I should have received mine own with usury.

Take therefore the talent from him, and give it unto him which hath ten talents.

For unto every one that hath shall be given, and he shall have abundance: but from him that hath not shall be taken away even that which he hath.

And cast ye the unprofitable servant into outer darkness: there shall be weeping and gnashing of teeth.

Matthew 25:14-30

In this amazing story, Jesus gave seven amazing points that would stand as eternal points of regret. There is no need to go to heaven to find out what will be important on Judgment Day. You can find out right now. You can believe the prophecies and predictions that Jesus gave about weeping and gnashing of teeth. Every time Jesus spoke of weeping and gnashing of teeth, He was warning Christians of what they would regret in eternity.

This passage is one of the most important guiding posts in our run-up to eternity. You must believe every single word as though someone rose up from the dead and came to tell you what will happen at the Judgment Seat of Christ.

For Jesus to have used the words "weeping and gnashing of teeth" you must appreciate the gravity of His warning. These are the things to watch out for. These are the things that will be painful to hear about on Judgment Day. These are the things that will make us regret and wish we could rush back to earth to do some more. Do you want to get to heaven and wish that you could come back to do some more? I hope not!

One day I had an experience with someone who had worked for me for several years. I later discovered that the person was treacherous. This individual criticised me, attacked me and vilified me in a way I never thought was possible. After the person was exposed and judged and forgiven, this person longed to be trusted and loved as he had been in the past. But I thought to myself that it would take another twenty years to develop that kind of trust again. A whole season had passed and it was not easy to go back in time and restart our lives.

When we get to heaven, many people will have this experience. They will discover how great God is. They will discover how supreme, excellent, real and wonderful He is. They will say, "O, I really love you. Please let me prove it. Please give me another chance to prove my love for you." Unfortunately, the season for living on earth would have been over. It would be impossible to go back to the earth and live another forty-three or more years to prove to God that you love Him.

Dear friend, this is your chance to prove that you love God. If you miss this great opportunity on the earth, you will weep and gnash your teeth for all eternity. Let the message of this book sink into your soul. This is the message of weeping and gnashing! These are points of eternal regret! These are things you should look out for! Things you should prepare for! Eternity awaits us all! Let us enter eternity without weeping and gnashing our teeth.

Six Points of Eternal Regret

1. You will eternally regret being slothful.

His lord answered and said unto him, Thou wicked and slothful servant, thou knewest that I reap where I sowed not, and gather where I have not strawed:

Matthew 25:26

Ministry involves hard work. You cannot do much for God if you are lazy. I have come to see that it is only hard-working people who accomplish much in the ministry. One of the commonest causes for fruitlessness is plain old laziness! Lazy people will be weeping and gnashing their teeth in heaven.

2. You will eternally regret being wicked.

His lord answered and said unto him, Thou wicked and slothful servant, thou knewest that I reap where I sowed not, and gather where I have not strawed:

Matthew 25:26

Doing nothing is wickedness! That is why Jesus called the man who did nothing with his talent a "wicked and unprofitable" servant. The words "wicked servant" have a profound meaning, deeper than we may care to meditate on. If you do nothing with the talent that God has given you, it may cause many people to go to hell; and that is wickedness! Avoid being called a wicked servant by using your talents, your gifts and your calling.

There will be weeping and gnashing of teeth because of your wickedness.

3. You will eternally regret not valuing the one talent given to you by God.

Take therefore the talent from him, and give it unto him which hath ten talents. For unto every one that hath shall be given, and he shall have abundance: but from him that hath not shall be taken away even that which he hath.

Matthew 25:28-29

Jesus predicted that those who did not use their talents would spend time weeping and gnashing their teeth. The gentleman who received one talent did not use his talent. He assumed that this talent would not yield much. In other words, he despised what he had been given. Many people feel they cannot preach as well as some of the well-known preachers of the world.

Perhaps you think that you can never have a large church. Perhaps, you feel you have just been given some bland, featureless gift. You complain because there is nothing remarkable about your gift. For this reason, you simply tuck it out of sight. Do not despise your one talent. It is good enough to do the job. You will eternally regret the fact that you did not use the one talent God has given you.

4. You will eternally regret being afraid. You will regret your fears.

And I was afraid, and went and hid thy talent in the earth: lo, there thou hast that is thine.

Matthew 25:25

Fear is an evil spirit which paralyses Christians into inactivity. Perhaps, it is one of the greatest forces that keeps people from taking up their talents and using them. At many junctions of my life, fear attempted to paralyze me into inactivity and fruitlessness. I can remember several times when fear tried to keep me from serving God and using my talents. It is very important to overcome your fears since they will keep you from using your talents or obeying the call from God.

Do not allow fear to keep you from obeying the call. Fear is an evil spirit! Do not follow an evil spirit! Follow the Holy Spirit! If you do not heed the simple warning not to follow your fears, you will only have yourself to blame. You will be weeping and gnashing your teeth in heaven for being afraid of serving God.

5. You will regret finding fault with leaders. You will regret accusing good leaders of being hard men.

Then he which had received the one talent came and said, Lord, I knew thee that thou art an hard man, reaping where thou hast not sown, and gathering where thou hast not strawed:

Matthew 25:24

Those who find fault and criticize pastors will weep and gnash their teeth for all eternity. Jesus has issued a stern warning about this. You find fault and criticize God's servants at your own risk. The gentleman with one talent did nothing because he found fault with the master who had sent him forth. He described him *as a hard man* who *benefitted* from things *he did not deserve*.

Fault-finding is a common characteristic of fruitless and inactive people! Instead of getting involved in the work of God, they sit back and analyse others who are fighting hard to do something for God. It is not difficult to find fault with someone if you are looking for faults.

The faults you find will only become the reason for you to withhold your own abilities. Why even bother to look for faults in God's servant? God did not choose angels to work for Him. He chose flaw-ridden men and women of varying backgrounds to do His work. You will always find something wrong when you look closely at God's servants. Protect yourself from fault-finding and criticizing. It will be an eternal point of regret.

6. You will regret hiding your gifts and talents.

And I was afraid, and went and hid thy talent in the earth: lo, there thou hast that is thine.

Matthew 25:25

Many people conceal who they are and what they can do. No one knows their potential because it is well concealed. Have you hidden your talents and gifts? Perhaps, fear of criticism has caused you to hide your gifts of singing, teaching, or even giving.

If you hide your gift, you will regret it forever. Jesus has predicted that people will weep and gnash their teeth for hiding their talents. You have received a direct and clear warning about the weeping and gnashing of teeth. Make sure that you do not fall into any of these mistakes. You cannot blame Jesus for not warning you.

CHAPTER 6

The Fifth Prophecy of Weeping and Gnashing

STRIVE TO ENTER IN AT THE STRAIT GATE: FOR MANY, I SAY UNTO YOU, WILL SEEK TO ENTER IN, AND SHALL NOT BE ABLE. When once the master of the house is risen up, and hath shut to the door, and ye begin to stand without, and to knock at the door, saying, Lord, Lord, open unto us; and he shall answer and say unto you, I know you not whence ye are: Then shall ye begin to say, We have eaten and drunk in thy presence, and thou hast taught in our streets. BUT HE SHALL SAY, I TELL YOU, I KNOW YOU NOT WHENCE YE ARE; DEPART FROM ME, ALL YE workers of iniquity. THERE SHALL BE WEEPING AND GNASHING OF TEETH, when ye shall see Abraham, and Isaac, and Jacob, and all the prophets, in the kingdom of God, and you yourselves thrust out. And they shall come from the east, and from the west, and from the north, and from the south, and shall sit down in the kingdom of God. And, behold, there are last which shall be first, and there are first which shall be last.

Luke 13:24-30

1. **You will regret not being with the minority who entered in through the narrow gate.**

   Strive to enter in at the strait [*narrow*] gate: for many, I say unto you, will seek to enter in, and shall not be able.

   Luke 13:24

On this earth, frivolous and deceptive things are popular. The masses follow emptiness, shallowness, jollity and inconsequentiality.

Jesus predicted that the masses would pass through the broad gate, following unimportant, insignificant, petty and trivial things. The masses will pass through the broad gate following the devil blindly into damnation.

Jesus predicted that many people would regret going on the broad way. They will regret not choosing the clearly marked narrow gate that leads to life.

Jesus prophesied that there would be weeping and gnashing of teeth because people followed the crowd and did what was . popular, rather than what was right.

Do you want to regret for the rest of eternity, that you followed the crowd rather than following the Lord?

I remember a brother who followed an evil man for many years and got destroyed in a terrible way. After being destroyed, this individual was weeping and gnashing his teeth for having trusted a deceiver for so long. Unfortunately, following this evil man led to many terrible judgments and consequences.

Being deceived is no reason to be excused from judgment. Adam and Eve were deceived by the serpent but they were still judged with a terrible judgment that we are all reeling under today.

Dear friend, you must guard your heart against the deception of following emptiness, shallowness, triviality and worthlessness. Do not be deceived by shining and glittering things. God does not care about man's opinion. Do not try to please men. Do not try to follow the crowd!

2. You will regret not knowing the Lord in reality for yourself.

> When once the master of the house is risen up, and hath shut to the door, and ye begin to stand without, and to knock at the door, saying, Lord, Lord, open unto us; and he shall answer and say unto you, I know you not whence ye are: Then shall ye begin to say, We have eaten and drunk in thy presence, and thou hast taught in our streets. But he shall say, I TELL YOU, I KNOW YOU NOT WHENCE YE ARE; depart from me, all ye workers of iniquity. THERE SHALL BE WEEPING AND GNASHING OF TEETH, when ye shall see Abraham, and Isaac, and Jacob, and all the prophets, in the kingdom of God, and you yourselves thrust out.
>
> Luke 13:25-28

Many Christians serve the Lord without knowing Him in reality. We must know the Lord! Not knowing God is the basis for being thrown out of heaven. Over the years, I have found that people that I do not know personally, but have sent out, do not do well on the mission field. I once called a group of twenty-five university students whom I did not know well and sent them on a mission. None of them really prospered or succeeded on the mission. After years of labour, I had to send people I knew to replace all of them.

In the ministry, knowing people is very important. Jesus uses His personal knowledge of you as a basis for judgment. One day, I met a brother who introduced himself as a pastor in one of my branch churches. I blurted out the words, "I don't know you." I had never seen him before and I had never heard of him. Being known is one of the highest qualifications for serving God.

Jesus predicted that many people would serve Him without knowing Him. Today, many Christians go to church but never read their Bibles or pray to God personally. Even more amazingly, Christians attend prayer meetings, shout in tongues and speak great words as they are led to, but do not have a personal relationship with God.

God has feelings! God has a personality! God knows those who know Him!

Can you imagine the regret we will feel after having participated in church services, congregational worship, tithe paying, Christian sacrifice only to be told that we do not know God and therefore must be cast away?

This is indeed an alarming prophecy.

3. You will eternally regret being a worker of iniquity.

But he shall say, I tell you, I know you not whence ye are; depart from me, all ye workers of iniquity

Luke 13:27

You will regret living in sin. You will regret not stepping away from a wretched life of wickedness and perversion. Do not continue living a twisted life, doing evil in secret. This sinful dark world is not your home. Come out and be separate, says the Lord (2 Corinthians 6:17).

Jesus predicted and prophesied that there would be people who would regret that they did not jump out of their sinful lifestyle. Do not wait until you are caught because you may never be caught whilst on earth.

4. You will regret being the first who becomes last instead of the last who becomes first.

And they shall come from the east, and from the west, and from the north, and from the south, and shall sit down in the kingdom of God. And, behold, there are last which shall be first, and there are first which shall be last.

Luke 13:29-30

The first shall be last and the last shall be first! Many people want to be first in this life. Following Jesus may mean you are last in the eyes of society. If you follow Jesus, you will be rejected by the seemingly important people.

If you follow Jesus, you will be rejected by the first, the prominent, the high and the mighty of your society. As you follow Jesus, you will be more associated with the last and insignificant in the world.

Jesus prophesied that many people would regret not accepting to be the last. Instead of accepting the rejection from high and mighty people, some Christians fight to join the elite, the powerful and the accepted ones.

Decide to accept your place in Christ. Do not fight to be accepted in the world and by the world. God will honour you by Himself. God will bless you and reward you in eternity. Be among the last today and you will be among the first in eternity!

CHAPTER 7

The Sixth Prophecy of Weeping and Gnashing

He answered and said unto them, He that soweth the good seed is the Son of man;

The field is the world; the good seed are the children of the kingdom; but the tares are the children of the wicked one; The enemy that sowed them is the devil; the harvest is the end of the world; and the reapers are the angels.

As therefore the tares are gathered and burned in the fire; so shall it be in the end of this world.

The Son of man shall send forth his angels, and they shall gather out of his kingdom all things that offend, and them which do iniquity; and shall cast them into a furnace of fire: THERE SHALL BE WAILING AND GNASHING OF TEETH. Then shall the righteous shine forth as the sun in the kingdom of their Father. Who hath ears to hear, let him hear.

Matthew 13:37-43

I n this section of scripture, Jesus uses the term, "wailing and gnashing" rather than "weeping and gnashing." In the Greek, the word "weeping" is exactly the same word as the word "wailing." The Greek word used here is "*klauthmos.*" Six times it is translated "weeping," and two times it is translated "wailing." However, both of these phrases mean the same thing. The important point is the gnashing. Gnashing of teeth is the highest sign of regret.

1. There will be eternal regret when you are told that you were a tare among the wheat.

The presence of tares is one of the worrying realities of ministry. False brethren, fake ministers, perfect pretenders and impostors have filled both the pulpits and the pews. Jesus predicted that there would be wailing, weeping and gnashing of teeth because of the presence of tares.

The presence of something that is not real is offensive. It takes angelic power to remove such fake and unreal things from our midst. Jesus said He would send angels to remove things that offend and those that do iniquity.

Jesus said He would cast them into the fire. All false Christians, fake workers, phony pastors and bishops can expect to be cast into a fire of judgment. Jesus said that falsehood and deception are offensive. Their presence is negative. The presence of Judas, traitors, falsehood, deception, treachery is always negative. It compromises the unity and contaminates the fellowship.

All such people are tares amongst the wheat. Jesus prophesied against tares. He said they offend! He said they are workers of iniquity! He said all tares would suffer great regret for their falsehood and longstanding deception. Make sure you do not live a life of deception and untruth.

Tares are weeds that look just like wheat. Tares do not bear fruit whilst wheat bears fruit. Tares are so similar to wheat that it is almost impossible to distinguish them until the time of the fruit. If you care to look for a picture of tares and wheat, you will be amazed at how similar they are.

Indeed, there are many things in the kingdom of God which are phony and fake. As you read this book, you may be one of the phony and fake ministers who have posed as a righteous and good person for many years. It is God who knows your heart. Most people cannot determine whether you are wheat or just a tare.

Over the years, I have become more sure that few of us have true discernment. We are completely hoodwinked by fake and false things. Evil men are applauded and hailed as men of integrity, honesty and goodness. Wicked women are praised as angels sent from God. These people are hailed because men do not know any better. We judge from the outward appearance and are completely wrong about most of our assessments. We know in part and we understand in part! Unfortunately, we know only a part of the truth about people.

The good, the bad and the ugly look the same. It is time to stop judging and assessing people by the little we know. Jesus was someone who would not judge by the seeing of the eyes and the hearing of the ears. God had given Him the Spirit of counsel and might (Isaiah 11:2,3).

2. The apostle Paul also warned us not to judge before the time.

Therefore do not go on passing judgment before the time, but wait until the Lord comes who will both bring to light the things hidden in the darkness and disclose the motives of men's hearts; and then each man's praise will come to him from God.

1 Corinthians 4:5 (NASB)

It is important that you judge yourself today. God has a special plan for the tares that are mixed up with the wheat. God has started a big fire to burn the tares and judge them severely.

CHAPTER 8

The Seventh Prophecy of Weeping and Gnashing

Again, the kingdom of heaven is like unto a net, that was cast into the sea, and gathered of every kind: Which, when it was full, they drew to shore, and sat down, and gathered the good into vessels, but cast the bad away.

So shall it be at the end of the world: the angels shall come forth, and sever the wicked from among the just, And shall cast them into the furnace of fire: THERE SHALL BE WAILING AND GNASHING OF TEETH.

Matthew 13:47-50

J esus prophesied that there would be a huge net that would gather all the fish from the sea. You and I are the fish that have been fished out of the waters. Unfortunately, not all the fish that have been caught in the net will be hauled ashore. Some of the fish drawn out of the sea will be thrown away.

Jesus prophesied that some people would be rejected. Some people will be considered unacceptable. There will be weeping and gnashing of teeth if you are rejected. What will be the basis of you being rejected? The good will be accepted and the bad will be rejected. Make sure you are not rejected.

Will God consider you as bad? Will you be considered as a bad minister? Will you be considered as a bad Christian? Will you be considered as something that is not genuine? There will be eternal regret if you are rejected as bad!

Conclusion

To the making of many books there is no end!

This book has issued to all of us seven warnings about weeping and gnashing of teeth. Allow the Holy Spirit to lead you away from all these things that will cause you to weep and gnash your teeth in regret one day.

The Lord is delivering you from a painful judgment! May you hear good news on the Judgment Day!